PAWSITIVE IMPACT

In the pages of "Tails of Devotion", lovingly brought to life by Dog Furiendly and Ralph & Co, every story shared is a step towards a world where every dog is cherished. This isn't just a collection of heartwarming tales; it's a powerful gesture of love extending to dogs in every corner of the UK and beyond.

By picking up this book, you've done more than just treat yourself to a treasury of canine adventures. You've lent a helping hand to charities like Hope Rescue, Many Tears, and Wild at Heart, each passionately working to brighten the lives of dogs who haven't had the easiest start. Imagine the wagging tails and bright eyes, all because you chose to be part of this journey.

So, as you chuckle and tear up reading these tales, remember the good you're spreading. Thank you for joining in this ripple of love and care, helping us ensure every dog gets their chance at a happy ending.

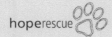

CONTENTS

Bean Goes to the Moon

A Story By Alex Kingsley

Every night, Bean would put on her pyjamas and listen to a bedtime story read by Bean's mother. After the story, she would look up at the night sky and make a wish upon a star. Bean made the same wish every night—to visit the moon.

Tonight was very different for Bean. She put on her pyjamas and listened to her mother read her a bedtime story. Afterwards, she went to her window and saw a shooting star fly across the sky. She wished again to one day go to the moon.

All of a sudden, a spaceship landed in her back yard. Bean could not believe her eyes. She ran outside in her pyjamas and approached the ship. Two dogs in astronaut suits hopped out and said, "We heard you make a wish, and we are here to make it come true."

Bean's mother heard all the commotion and came outside. Bean asked for her permission to go to the moon with the astronauts who came to bring her dream to life. Her mother packed them all snacks and wished them luck on their long journey, being sure to remind them Bean had to be back for her bedtime. The astronauts gave Bean a spacesuit to put over her pyjamas, and off they went, flying into outer space.

They sailed around the solar system, visiting all the planets. They even showed Bean the stars she had been wishing on. A giant meteor whizzed past their ship, and there it was—the moon was straight ahead. Bean was bursting with glee. They landed beside a crater and opened up the door.

All three pups hopped out of their ship and ran around the moon. They jumped, skipped, floated, and twirled their ways across the moon, playing. The astronauts could not believe how much time had passed while having fun. They checked their watches, and it was 10 minutes until Bean's bedtime!

They all scurried back to the ship, tired from all the excitement, and turned on all the controls. They said goodnight to the moon, the planets, and all of the stars, then zoomed back down to Earth to bring Bean home. They landed in her back yard just in time for bed, where Bean's mum was waiting for her with some fresh, clean pyjamas.

"Did you make it to the moon?" she asked the space travellers. They all looked at each other and smiled. "We made it to the moon and saw the entire galaxy." Bean's wish had finally come true.

Ivan's Tail

A Story By Katrina Rohman

Once upon a time, there lived a canine adventurer named Ivan. Ivan wasn't just any dog; he was a rescue pup with a tale as remarkable as his wagging tail. He came from a faraway place called Bosnia, in a gloomy shelter where hope seemed hard to find, wondering if he'd ever get a chance to explore the world beyond the rusty bars. Then, one day, two superheroes in raincoats and walking boots arrived. Katrina and Michael were on a mission to save the day, and Ivan was their chosen sidekick.

As soon as Ivan landed in the enchanting land of Cardiff, he knew he was in for a treat. Katrina and Michael's home was like a palace for a pup, complete with plush beds and toys galore. With newfound confidence, Ivan began his Cardiff conquest.

The trio started their adventures by visiting the local pubs. Ivan quickly became the talk of the town with his irresistible charm and love for belly rubs. Even the grumpiest patrons couldn't resist his furry charisma. The pubs turned into Ivan's personal meet-and-greet spots, and he became Cardiff's unofficial canine ambassador.

Restaurants soon followed on Ivan's social calendar. With a taste for adventure and impeccable table manners, he became a regular at the city's finest dining establishments. Ivan's palate was more refined than most humans', and he could critique a steak with a discerning bark.

But Cardiff was just the beginning. One weekend, Katrina and Michael decided it was time for a grand staycation. They packed their bags and Ivan's favourite treats, setting off for the picturesque land of Cornwall.

The trio explored the charming coastal villages, strolled along sandy beaches, and chased seagulls in the crisp sea breeze. Ivan discovered the joy of digging in the sand and promptly declared himself the king of the beach. Even the seagulls couldn't argue with that royal decree.

Cornwall had more surprises in store. The walks became epic adventures as Ivan encountered fluffy sheep who seemed unimpressed by his canine antics. The trio explored ancient castles, and Ivan couldn't help but imagine himself as the valiant knight guarding the kingdom.

As the sun dipped below the horizon, painting the sky in hues of orange and pink, Ivan, Katrina, and Michael found themselves grateful for the laughter, joy, and love they'd discovered together.

And so, every night in Cardiff, under the twinkling stars, Ivan curled up in his plush bed, dreaming of the incredible adventures that awaited him in the world beyond. The once-rescue pup had become a legend, a furry ambassador of love, proving that every dog's tale deserves a happy ending. And Ivan's was just getting started.

Snow

A Story By Cheri Atrill

Mavis is a puppy who lives on a farm. She has lots of friends to play with on her farm: Henry the hedgehog, Lola the lamb, Maddie the duckling, Barney the owl, and many more.

One cold autumn afternoon, Mavis was curled up in front of the warm fire when she heard Henry calling her from the barn. "Mavis, come quick," he said. Mavis went running out to the barn to see what was wrong. When she arrived, she found Henry, Lola, Maddie, and Barney all cuddled together. "What's the matter?" said Mavis. "There are cold white leaves falling from the sky," said Lola. It had been snowing at the farm, and they had never seen snow before. Mavis popped her head out of the barn door and saw the snow falling to the ground.

"Where are the white leaves coming from?" said Maddie. "There are no trees in the sky." Mavis was very curious about the white leaves, so she decided to go outside to investigate. By this time, the snow had covered the farm and the trees around them. "These are not leaves," Mavis shouted to her friends in the barn. "Then what is it?" Barney asked. "I'm not sure," Mavis answered, "but it's very cold on my paws."

Henry, Maddie, Lola, and Barney weren't as brave as Mavis, so they watched her from the warmth of the barn. Mavis took a few more curious steps in the cold white snow. "Mavis, are you okay?" It was Henry's mum, Mrs. Hog. "No, Mrs. Hog," Mavis answered. "The farm has turned white and cold, and there are white leaves falling from the sky."

"It's snowing, Mavis," Mrs. Hog laughed as she answered. "Where are the others?" "They are all in the barn," said Mavis. Mrs. Hog and Mavis went back to the barn. "What are you all doing inside the barn?" Mrs. Hog asked the friends. "We are staying away from the cold, scary white leaves," said Henry. "It's snowing, Henry. Snow isn't scary," Mrs. Hog replied as she took his hand and walked to the barn door. The other curious friends followed. "The snow is fun. Why don't you all go outside together and see?"

The friends stepped out of the barn slowly, one by one. They could feel the snow crunching under their feet. "It's very soft," said Lola. "It's making my beak cold," Maddie replied. Mavis was feeling brave and decided to put her face in the snow. When she looked up, she had snow all over her nose and face. The friends all fell over laughing. "My mum was right," said Henry. "The snow is fun."

"Mavis"... "Mavis," Mavis's humans were calling her. It was time for Mavis to head home. It was getting late and time for bed. "Bye, friends, see you tomorrow," Mavis shouted as she ran up to the farmhouse. After a long day of exploring the snow, Mavis curled up in front of the warm fire, ready to dream of her next big adventure.

Scrump and the friendship Stone

A Story By Emrys Scott-Whalley

Once upon a time, in a cosy village nestled between lush green hills and sparkling streams, lived two adorable terriers named Scrump and Gwen. Scrump, a little black terrier with a wagging tail, and Gwen, a black and tan terrier with kind, soulful eyes, were the best of friends.

Every evening, as the stars twinkled in the sky and the moon cast its gentle glow, Scrump and Gwen would meet under the old oak tree near the village square. It was their special place, where they shared stories, giggles, and dreams.

One starry night, as they settled beneath the oak tree, Gwen spoke softly, "Scrump, have you ever wondered about the magic of friendship?"

Scrump tilted his head, his eyes wide with curiosity. "What's so magical about it, Gwen?"

Gwen smiled warmly. "Friendship is like a shining star in the sky. It lights up our lives, brings joy, and makes every moment special."

Eager to explore this magical idea, Scrump asked, "How can we make our friendship even more magical, Gwen?"

Gwen's eyes twinkled with an idea. "Let's embark on a quest to find the Friendship Stone, said to possess the purest magic of all. It's said to grant wishes that make friendships stronger and hearts happier."

Excited about the adventure, Scrump and Gwen set off on their quest. Through fields of wildflowers, across babbling brooks, and under the moonlit sky, they journeyed in search of the fabled Friendship Stone.

Their quest led them to a meadow where a wise old owl named Ollie resided. Ollie perched atop a branch and greeted them with a hoot.

"Ah, little adventurers," hooted Ollie, "seeking the magic of friendship, are you?" Gwen nodded eagerly. "Yes, wise Ollie. Do you know where we can find the Friendship Stone?"

Ollie blinked thoughtfully. "The path to the Friendship Stone lies within your hearts. It's in the moments you share, the laughter you bring, and the care you show for each other."

With Ollie's wisdom guiding them, Scrump and Gwen realized that the real magic of friendship was in their togetherness, their support, and the joy they found in each other's company.

As they returned to their cosy corner under the oak tree, Scrump and Gwen curled up together, feeling the warmth of their friendship. They gazed at the twinkling stars, knowing that they had found the true magic of friendship within themselves.

And as the moon smiled down on them, the village whispered stories of Scrump and Gwen—two inseparable friends who discovered that the greatest magic was the love and kindness they shared with each other.

Daisy The Moo

A Story By Louisa O'Brien

Once upon a time, there was a puppy called Daisy. Daisy lived with her human Mum and Dad and her puppy sister Lucy. Now, although Lucy and Daisy were most definitely puppies, Daisy truly believed she was a cow!

You see, Daisy got her name from her Dad. Who when he first saw her, with her floppy, fluffy ears and her little waggy tail, he noticed she had the resemblance of a little baby cow. Daisy was all white with just three blobs of black, and that's when her Dad said, "We'll call her Daisy, Daisy the moo cow, now there's no going back."

Although she ate puppy food, she also grazed on grass. Daisy might have barked too, but it mostly came out as a moo!

One day, Lucy had enough of Daisy's nonsense, so she turned to her and said, "Listen, Daisy, you're not a moo cow, you are a puppy!"

Daisy sat and tilted her head.

Puzzled, she asked, "Moo?"

Lucy knew that Daisy should not "moo," and luckily she knew exactly what to do. "Come with me, Daisy, I've got something to show you." Off she plodded, and Daisy followed too!

Through the garden, they walked, then out the garden gate. They were in quite a rush as they couldn't be back too late. They hopped into the field and under the fence until they finally reached the place that Lucy had meant.

They entered a field. With long grass and cowpats. Until they wandered up to 3 big cows all in straw hats.

"Nice to meet moo," the biggest cow said to Lucy and Daisy.

Daisy couldn't believe her eyes. These big cows really took her by surprise!

They stayed in the field all day long, they sang, danced, and played until Daisy realised she was wrong!

"It's been really lovely to meet you, Mrs Cow, but I've just realised the time, and we've got to go now," said Daisy.

As they walked back home, excited for their dinners, Daisy said to Lucy, "I'm not a cow after all. I'm not that round, and I woof, I don't moo, but I had such a wonderful day, and it's all thanks to you!"

Nice to meet Moo..

Whiskers, Wings, and Wagging Tails

A Story By Melodie Tardif-Faessel

In a quaint village nestled amongst rolling hills, there stood an ancient castle, surrounded by lush gardens. Here begins the tale of Elliot, a light fluffy Golden Retriever, known for his kind heart, gentle nature, and boundless curiosity.

One sunny morning, Elliot wandered into the castle gardens for an adventure with his humans, his nose twitching with excitement. He was immediately captivated by the array of colourful flowers that filled the air with their sweet fragrance. As Elliot trotted along the winding paths, he encountered a group of squirrels. These squirrels, playful and chatty, shared stories of their escapades in the garden, from finding the juiciest acorns to playing hide and seek among the leaves.

As he ventured further, Elliot stumbled upon a group of splendid pheasants. These elegant birds, with their richly coloured feathers, spoke of the changing seasons and the beauty of the garden throughout the year. They described the snow-covered branches in winter and the lush greenery in spring, painting a picture of the garden's ever-changing charm.

In the afternoon's mild warmth, Elliot found himself by a serene pond, where ducks and swans glided gracefully on the water. They told Elliot about life on the pond, from the soft ripples of the water to the joy of teaching their young ones to swim. Elliot listened intently, fascinated by their different perspectives on life in the castle grounds.

In a secluded part of the garden, Elliot met a mother deer and her fawn. They spoke softly of their life in the woods, a world of quiet grazing and cautious exploration, offering Elliot a glimpse of the forest's serene existence.

Wandering further, Elliot stumbled upon a cat lounging in the sun. The cat, with its sleek fur and posed demeanour, spoke of its solitary adventures, from climbing lofty branches to stealthily navigating the garden, embodying a life of independence and grace.

As the day neared its end, Elliot's path crossed with a big, fluffy Newfoundland named Samson. Samson, with his gentle manner and friendly wag, shared stories of his own adventures within the vast gardens, creating an immediate bond between the two dogs. In the forest clearing, they played together, their joyful barks and playful antics echoing around the trees, creating a moment of pure, unbridled joy.

As the sky turned to hues of orange and pink, casting a golden glow over the garden, Elliot heard his humans calling him. They told him it was time to leave and promised a delicious dinner waiting at home. Reluctantly, Elliot bid farewell to his new friends, his heart full of the day's adventures and the stories of life in the gardens.

Elliot's adventure in the castle gardens is a reminder of the wonders that lie in the simple pleasures of nature and the joy of making new friends, regardless of their shape or size. As he trotted home, his tail wagging happily, he looked forward to more adventures in the days to come.

River

A Story By Simona King

"River, let's go," my human said. I excitedly wagged my tail and let out a little yelp of joy; those words usually mean something fun is about to happen. I sat down patiently as I waited for my lead to be clipped onto my collar.

My human took me to the car and opened the boot. "Up, up," said my human while tapping my bed. I leaped up, anticipating where we may be going. The park? The woods? The beach? After what seemed like hours, we finally arrived.

I didn't recognise this place; the surroundings were different, and the smells were new. I hadn't been here before. It was such a stunning autumn evening with bright, vivid colours everywhere! As we followed the path out of the car park, I could see this beautiful meadow with luscious green grass. In the distance, I could see a line of trees; I couldn't wait for the different smells I was going to experience. My human sat me down and asked me to wait. She unclipped my lead and pulled something out of her pocket. I tilted my head; it was my SQUEAKY TENNIS BALL! I love my squeaky tennis ball. I suddenly sprung from my sit position and did an eager tap dance. I carefully mirrored the ball as my owner waved it around. "Throw it! Throw it!" I was telling her. Then she did! I let my excitement fuel my speed as I chased after it. In one bounce, I caught it and brought it back to my human. This is my favourite game!

My human threw the ball as we walked through the meadow. I was too focused on catching my ball to notice any of my surroundings. We continued to play fetch on our journey towards the trees.

We were close to the line of trees now. I abruptly picked up a scent; it was too good not to follow. I dropped my ball and swiftly weaved through the trees. I could hear my human shout words, but my nose had taken over all my senses. I continued to follow my nose, dodging trees and ducking through bushes. The urge was just too strong; I made my way deeper into the thick forest.

After following the scent for a while, I decided this scent was no longer interesting and thought it would be best to return to my human. I turned around and noticed I was in a completely different place. I could no longer see the meadow nor my human. I panned my head, scanning my surroundings. All I could see was trees, lots of them. I suddenly realised I didn't know which direction I came from. I tilted my ears, trying to pick up my human's voice... nothing.

I felt so small, so alone.

I searched the area but couldn't find my human. It started to get dark, and the wind howled. I was desperate to get back to my human now. But I was tired, my nose and legs were exhausted. I decided it was best to get some rest. I retreated under a fallen tree where the roots were exposed; it was enough to keep me slightly sheltered. I curled up and slightly closed my eyes.

I heard rustling close by, which made me realise I had fallen asleep. I quickly opened my eyes; it was pitch black now, and I was encountered by a curious fox.

"What are you doing here?" said the fox.

"I'm lost," I replied.

"Well, this is my territory; you don't belong here," snarled the fox.

"I'm sorry, I'm just looking for my human," I said timidly.

"Human? Ha, you're a measly pet," the fox laughed. "You better get out of here, or there'll be trouble!"

"I don't mean any harm," I said gently.

"I said, get away!" The fox growled.

The fox lunged at me. I managed to dodge his attack and darted away into the long night.

For hours, I scoured through the scary dark woods in search of my human. I just couldn't find her. Realisation started to sink in; what if this is forever? What if I'll never find her again? My train of thought was interrupted by the sound of my belly rumbling. It made me think of home. My nice warm bed, my favourite toys, my tasty breakfasts and dinners, my human snuggles and cuddles. What if that was all gone?

The sun started to rise. I could tell it was early morning; I had been wandering for many hours, and my paws became so sore. I was starting to lose hope. I looked up to the sky and focused on the sound of chirping birds. The peaceful sound was interrupted by something approaching me. Filled with fear, I cowered to the floor, closing my eyes. The sound of crunching leaves got closer and louder. Suddenly, I heard, "Oh my... RIVER!" I opened my eyes... It was my human. She'd found me! I found myself frozen in this cowered position. I was no longer scared, but an overwhelming feeling of guilt rushed through me. I was the one who ran away. I abandoned my owner to chase a silly scent. Was she mad at me? All these questions filled my head. I could sense the adrenaline radiating off my human as she swiftly leaned down and wrapped her arms around me. A sense of relief sunk into both of us. I kissed every inch of her face, all of a sudden tasting something salty? She was crying. Was she sad? I was confused for a second, but she was smiling. She was happy. I was happy. "I found you, I was so worried," she said as she grasped me tighter. I was finally safe in my human's arms, I was finally home.

Bentley's Belly

A Story By Helen Mills

Bentley loved food, not liked, loved!

His tummy was so vast that with each new mouthful, the spots on his coat were never the same size. As the days and months rolled by, the Dalmatian ate more and more and more. His long-suffering owner, Dora, despaired at his expanding appetite, but Bentley could not help himself. One more bone became two, and three little dog biscuits became four. Soon, Bentley was the largest dog in the neighbourhood. His steps grew smaller, the yawns wider, and the gambolling so slow and arduous, he could gambol no more. Bentley's belly bonanza was growing wildly out of hand. Even his loyal canine companion, Titch, was losing hope.

One cold and drizzly afternoon, Dora returned from a trip into town, hung up her coat in the porch as usual, and went to see her beloved Dalmatian. Underneath her arm was a very large dog bed, extremely plush and twice the size of Bentley...it needed to be. "You'll eat me out of house and home!" she sighed, placing the new dog bed under the wooden staircase.

Bentley soon lost interest in Dora's latest acquisition and was far more concerned with the pockets of her smock top, which he knew contained the last of yesterday's treats. Yet perhaps Bentley should have paid more attention to the new addition under the stairs, for when night fell, there was an eeriness to the house and a distinct lack of warmth as the last embers of the fire blacked out. Something was amiss. Bentley, who felt an incredible unease, was just about to leave his plush new bed when it began to hover in mid-air. Bentley woofed as loudly as he could, but Dora was fast asleep, and the levitating dog soon zoomed out of the porch door and into the frozen outdoors. The startled Dalmatian travelled across the starry night sky, above rooftops and billowing chimneys. "Where is this thing taking me?" cried Bentley. As the biting wind grew frostier still, he could do nothing but snuggle down in his bed and close his large brown eyes.

As he blinked, the sun poured over Bentley and gradually roused him. The scenery was unfamiliar; a little cottage surrounded by a canopy of tall and threatening trees. Feeling cold and lonely, he trudged along, shifting his vast body with him. The door was ajar, just wide enough to allow Bentley to enter. His eyes widened immediately. Dog bones hung from the hallway like a chandelier, and everywhere he turned, he could see tasty treats and his favourite, meaty chews. The Dalmatian blinked again, expecting to wake from this dream, but everything was real. Within minutes, Bentley had devoured a significant portion of the house, which was completely edible and completely delicious. He gorged himself for hours until his belly could hold no more!

But as the day drew to a close, his appetite might have been sated, but there were no late-night cuddles from Dora and no sign of his best friend little Titch to tell him goodnight. The dog bed was still outside, and Bentley could not even move to lie back on it. The cold reality of his gluttony hurt and ached as much as his stomach, and he began to cry. As soon as his tears touched the enchanted cottage, the dog bed zoomed through the door, what was left of it, and landed right in front of

Bentley. Struggling with all his canine might, he scooped up his belly and dived into the soft, cushiony fabric. Still fearful of heights, he closed his eyes as the bed once more whisked him away.

"Come on, Bentley, it's time to play!" said Titch excitedly, prancing around him like a pony rather than a dog! Then suddenly, Dora appeared with a bowl of breakfast for her beloved Dalmatian. For the first time in Bentley's life, he did not feel hungry, not even slightly, not even at all. Instead, he brushed his furry and spotty coat against his owner and looked up at her with a humble heart.

From that moment on, Bentley shunned his greedy ways and went for more walks with Dora and Titch. The weight soon disappeared, and all became well. As for the magical dog bed, Bentley continued to sleep in it, yet it never took him on any more adventures, and it lay peacefully where it was always meant to be, under the wooden staircase, in the warm and with Bentley inside, sound asleep.

The Best Boy

A Story By Jodie Louza

Noah felt the crisp and unforgiving wintery air ricochet against his nose, forcing him to open his eyes. He inspected his surroundings, his bright eyes flickering back and forth like candles burning intensely on a cosy evening. Noah didn't know the luxury of a warm, peaceful night. His liquorice black ears twitched. *What was that?* Hopefully not that elephantine dog from a few nights ago, returning to wreak havoc. It had taken Noah a long time to secure this abandoned apartment. It was absent of furniture, family, or food, but it was his home. Noah wasn't the biggest of dogs, but he could hold his own - he had the scars to prove it. Anything to survive.

The vibration below intensified, and it became clear that this was more than just one rival. It sounded like a pack. Noah's fur began to stand on end, as a tidal wave of fear engulfed him. It was always worse at night. Noah was drowsy, his guard was down. He wasn't successful in scoring an evening meal today. He needed rest.

Noah's pounding heart was almost as thunderous as the footsteps that were now encroaching upon him. *There's no way these dogs are taking my...* Noah's train of thought was curtly interrupted by an alien voice breaking the tension. "Let's go through here." *Humans?*

Some humans were good. They offered scraps of food and rubbed Noah's tummy, making him feel appreciated for a minuscule moment. They assured him he was a "good boy", but if that was the case, why did they all leave him to fend for himself?

Noah dreamt of being a true "good boy." He regularly caught glimpses of this distant desire. The "good boys" paraded around town with their humans by their side, radiating mutual joy. They lived in occupied illuminated buildings, with regular mealtimes and space to play, and an inviting place to rest their heads at night. Good boys had love. Noah longed to be loved.

"Oh, look at that little dog over there! Poor thing."
Less of the little, human.

Noah was apprehensive. These humans looked and smelt okay...but you could never really know for sure.

"Come on little one, come over here."

Noah stayed put, unwilling to extend his trust to the humans. *What if this is a big mistake? What if this risk is the reason that I lose my home?* "He looks hungry. We should get him something to eat before we do anything else."

Noah could get on board with that. His stomach rumbled boisterously, his mouth salivating in anticipation. It was almost as if the "anything else" momentarily escaped from his usually tense mind...

The hum of scuffling paws and playful barking startled Noah. He prised open his eyes, his black button nose twitching to make sense of the morning as he shook last night's sleep away. A world of scents saturated the atmosphere. Noah was hit with the intense yet appealing combination of fresh air, earth, remnants of jellied meat, and canines. Lots of canines. It had been a good amount of weeks now, and Noah still felt astonished at the number of dogs that were living harmoniously -

but he liked it.

This new routine was...enjoyable. It lightened the weight on Noah's shoulders. Food was prepared reliably. Walks were long and stimulating, with acquaintances of both the dog and human variety congregating along the way. Noah had a reasonably comfortable place to lay at dusk. It was almost entirely dissimilar to his previous home, where responsibility was ever-growing and imperative for survival. One element that had not disappeared (aside from the inescapable cold), was the ache that Noah felt to be a fully-fledged member of a loving family, to be a "good boy".

The humans at this home were constantly rushed off their feet, scheduling, communicating, and rotating tasks to ensure that every dog was taken care of. Sometimes, visitor humans would arrive, which was always a thrilling event. Noah knew not to have high expectations. They were much like the humans in the streets, friendly but fickle, like birds pausing their daily routine to grab a quick refreshment before spreading their wings to take flight again.

At times, some dogs would leave with the visitors, wagging their tails enthusiastically while being met with a flurry of fuss and hope. *They must be the good ones.* Noah pondered, morosely resting his chin on his paws. He was yet to discover the formula to being "good".

"Come on, Noah! Shall we go and say hello, lovely?! Come on". Noah bared his teeth into a large, giddy smile as he felt the delight muster inside of his frame. Whether it was fleeting or not, attention was always welcome. I wonder what these visitors will be like? I hope they have a treat for me. He scampered along with his favourite caregiver, Jenny, who had a mirrored optimistic grin resting on her apple-like cheeks.

Noah could hear hushed yet animated tones as he approached two friendly-looking humans. In the pit of his stomach, he felt that ever-present longing intensify. It draped around him like a familiar fluffy blanket on a winter's night, ridding him of his apprehension and strife.

The couple looked youthful and kind, their eyes glistening like glitter as they knelt to greet Noah. Noah didn't want to wait to meet them. The emotions were too powerful – he was drawn to them. He bounded over, leaping in the air with glee in between pats and laughter. The feeling was mutual.

"Oh, he's absolutely wonderful!" the woman exclaimed, tears brimming from her empathetic eyes.

"He is." Noah nestled his head into the man's lap, clinging to his homely embrace. Everything he had ever dreamed of finally felt within reach. He had never had an urge to be so trustful. Noah felt sincerity radiating through these humans like never before. "He's the best boy."

The best boy? Even better than good?! I did it. I finally did it.

Spencer's Dreams

A Story By E M Varley

Once upon a time in a quaint town nestled between rolling hills and babbling brooks, there lived a fluffy little dog named Spencer. With fur as soft as a cloud and eyes that sparkled with mischief, Spencer was the heart and soul of the neighbourhood.

As the sun dipped below the horizon, casting a warm glow over the town, Spencer's ears perked up with anticipation. Nightfall was his favourite time because that's when the magical adventures would begin.

One evening, as the stars twinkled in the velvet sky, Spencer felt an irresistible urge to explore. He slipped out of the cosy house where he lived with his mum and ventured into the moonlit streets.

The night was alive with the symphony of crickets and the gentle rustle of leaves. Spencer's paws carried him to the heart of the town park, where an ancient oak tree stood strong. Underneath its branches, a group of woodland creatures gathered for a secret meeting.

To Spencer's surprise, they welcomed him with open arms—or rather, open paws. There was Nutmeg the squirrel, Whiskers the wise old rabbit, and Tinker the mischievous mouse. They were the guardians of the park at night when it became a magical place where dreams blossomed.

Spencer loved to make new friends, so he wagged his fluffy tail and got ready for the adventure that awaited him. The park at night was a hidden oasis, glowing with the soft light of enchanted fireflies. Flowers of every colour adorned the landscape, and a gentle breeze carried whispers of dreams.

Tinker, with a twinkle in his eyes, handed Spencer a tiny watering can. "Your job, Spencer, is to sprinkle a bit of your magic on these flowers. Your love and joy will make them bloom with dreams for everyone who sees them."

With a sense of purpose, Spencer pranced around, sprinkling his magic with every step. The flowers responded by releasing a burst of fragrance, carrying dreams and wishes into the night air.

As Spencer completed his task, the night came alive with a magical glow, and the woodland creatures cheered.

With a heart full of joy, Spencer bid his newfound friends farewell and made his way back home. His mum was still asleep, unaware of the magical transformation that had taken place.

As Spencer curled up in his cosy bed, he knew that his nightly adventures were not just dreams but a testament to the magic that happens when a little fluffy dog shares his love with the world. And so, under the watchful gaze of the moon, Spencer drifted into a peaceful slumber, ready for more enchanting escapades in the nights to come.

The Copycat

A Story By Max Chang

"Elliot! We're here."

The soothing symphony of rhythmic rumbles and whispering wheels was interrupted by the call. The dull clank of my seatbelt signalled that I stood up. My tail brushed against the backseat, leaving bits of fur with every wag. Upon visual inspection, the place appeared to be unfamiliar. Perhaps a new location for a walk?

"What do you think?"

I woofed excitedly, and they laughed as they opened their doors to step out. A waft of sweet and earthy aroma entered my nose. I extended my neck out of the car and took quick cursory sniffs. The smell of pinene and limonene suggested coniferous trees nearby.

"Stop pulling! I can't unclip you."

Once free, I dove into the fragrance and began my investigation. Each blade of grass eagerly shared their unique odours. There was an olfactory orchestra of earthy tones from the soil. Beneath the green notes, there was a subtle redolence of a dewy morning. A sharp acidic scent emitted from busy lines of ants nearby. As my nose hovered over their tiny procession, the gusts of air caused them to scatter in order to protect their precious cargo. I turned my attention and followed a recent musky scent in search of a hedgehog, only to have it disappear underneath a bush emitting a fresh leafy aroma.

"Elliot! Over here!"

I snapped around and dashed over, cutting through the resinous mist that permeated the lawn. Keys jingled, and the door swung open, its lower edge grazing against the wooden floor with a rough grating sound. A waft of artificial lemon-scented agents and the musty, sweet aged wood flooded out. Just as I bolted past the doorway, I noticed a pile of boxes directly in front of me. My legs frantically scrambled to get some grip on the slippery surface as my tail executed vigorous whirls to find equilibrium. In this flurry of motion, the momentum carried me straight into the boxes with a gentle thud.

"Careful, Elliot!"

As I prepared to wag my tail to assure my humans that I was unscathed, a crash caused me to jump. My earlier actions had disturbed the stability and caused a chain reaction that toppled the topmost box. While the cardboard muffled the impact, it was not enough to prevent the contents from spilling out, and created a blend of soft thumps and high-pitched squeals. All of it was overshadowed by the taps of a ball fervently making its escape. My ears perked, and I leaped into action, determined to catch my prey. I carefully skidded around the boxes and scattered toys, and bounded towards the hallway with only the sound of the lively hops to guide me.

The hallway stretched ahead, lined with empty shelves and small rugs, and the ball seemed to dance away from me, each bounce a taunting leap further down the corridor. I galloped after my prize, urged on by the beats of my paw pads. As I gained on the ball and prepared to snatch it with a well-timed pounce, I misjudged the distance and my nose collided with the ball, sending it further down the hall. Undeterred, I chased after the ball with renewed vigour. The ball zipped down the hallway and struck a door that was slightly ajar. With a dull and hollow sound, the energetic jounce was reduced to a few lethargic thumps. As the ball came to a rest, I gently picked up the ball and cheerfully gave it several squeezes.

A tantalising but familiar coniferous smell drifted through the doorway. Using my snout, I carefully pushed against the door which swung open smoothly to the right, revealing a room bathed in soft sunlight from the open window. My inquisitive gaze swept from left to right as I took in the surroundings. Suddenly, a startling sight caused me to drop my ball, jump backward, and retreat behind the door. Confusion set in as I tried to figure out how I could have missed detecting the presence of another dog. Could it be an intruder, a potential foe, or perhaps a new friend?

I strained my senses and could not perceive any scents, sounds, nor vibrations to confirm the existence of the unexplainable dog. Peeking cautiously around the door, I observed the other dog doing the same. From the corner of my eye, I noticed two balls. The creature possessed a friendly and quizzical appearance, accompanied by a pair of warm expressive eyes with a hint of wariness. Its ears, soft and slightly floppy, perked up inquisitively. The sleek black nose quivered with curiosity as it sampled the air. One side of the mouth was pulled back, exposing a few pristine white teeth, while the other side retained an amiable, relaxed position.

As I inched my way from behind the door to gain a clearer view, my actions were mimicked by the cautious canine. I stopped, and the copycat did the same. The gentle waves of this imitator's fur created a luxurious texture that shimmered in the sunlight. A set of sleek, muscular legs connected the strong shoulders to the fluffy paws.

With the same heedful approach, we both advanced closer. My nose continued to twitch with curiosity as there was still no scent of this emulator. A long and feathered golden plume came into view. We locked eyes and wagged our tails in unison. I took one step closer, still determined to see if this new companion was friendly. The other dog mirrored the movement but stopped when I did.

We slowly edged closer, noses nearly touching, eager to exchange a sniff. In an unexpected twist, my nose met a smooth, cool surface. We took a step back and tilted our heads as I examined the imprint and the faint steam left by my snout. With a sense of bewilderment, I carefully moved forward once more and sniffed again. The copycat. The two identical balls. Gradually, the realisation dawned - the mysterious dog right before my eyes is me!

Casper Helps a Friend

Story and Illustrations By Philippa Hutter

The sun was shining, and Casper was excited for the day. He jumped out of bed, gave a big stretch, and quickly ate his breakfast before walking over to the back door and poking his head out of the cat flap. The garden smelled of flowers and freshly cut grass, and Casper quickly pushed through the cat flap and ran outside.

As he began his daily sniff around the flower beds, he suddenly stopped as he saw a little face looking back at him from underneath the leaf of a sunflower. It was a little mouse.

"Oh hello," said Casper, "I've not seen you in my garden before. Where have you come from?"

"I'm very sorry for the intrusion," squeaked the mouse, "but I was looking for a new place to live. You see, someone has made a mess of my house, and I don't think I can live there anymore."

Casper felt very sad for the mouse. "That sounds terrible!" he said, "You are more than welcome to live here if you would like."

"Thank you very much, that's very kind of you," squeaked the mouse, "but what I would really love is to have my home back. I loved it so much."

"Won't you show me where you lived?" said Casper, "Maybe we can tidy up the mess for you."

With that, the mouse scurried toward the end of the garden with Casper following behind. At the bottom of the garden, the mouse scrambled up and over the fence, waiting at the top to check that Casper was also able to get through. Casper squeezed through a hole at the bottom of the fence, and both he and the mouse trotted along together until they reached the park.

The mouse led Casper to the corner of the park where there was a little mouse-sized house. There was a flower pot lying on its side where the mouse had piled up leaves, grass, and feathers to make a comfy bed, as well as lots of other nice places to hide.

However, right next to the mouse's house were empty metal cans which said 'lemonade' on the side, crisp packets, sandwich boxes, chocolate wrappers, and empty bags of sweets which had all been left by someone having a picnic.

"Oh no," said Casper, "look at all that rubbish which has been left, making a mess of your house! And those open metal cans look dangerously sharp!"

Although there was a lot of mess, Casper knew just what to do. He quickly ran over to a tree on the other side of the park and let out a "woof" as he barked to his friend Owl at the top of the tree. Owl swooped down to meet Casper, very happy to see his friend.

"Hello there, Casper. How are you today?" hooted Owl.

"I'm very well, thank you, Owl, but my new friend mouse is having some trouble, and I was wondering if you would be able to help us."

Owl followed Casper back to the mouse's house where Owl hooted in surprise at all the rubbish that had been left. As Casper nuzzled the rubbish into a pile, Owl quickly started picking it up with his feet and flying with it over to the bin. "I really cannot believe that people left all of this rubbish lying around," hooted Owl, "making such a mess of mouse's pretty home!"

Working together, Casper and Owl were able to soon clear up all the mess until the mouse's home was spotless. "Thank you both so much," squeaked the mouse, "I don't know what I would do without you."

"That's what friends are for," smiled Casper, "and I hope you will come and visit me again soon."

After saying goodbye, Owl flew back up to his tree, and Casper began to run home, squeezing under the fence and trotting back up the garden. "It's definitely time for lunch after all that cleaning," thought Casper, as he jumped through the cat flap.

"I'm very glad I was able to help my new friend," he thought, "but I do hope next time people are having a nice picnic in the park they remember not to leave their rubbish lying around. Otherwise, poor mouse will have nowhere nice to live anymore." With that, Casper heard his owner walking into the room and, going up to say hello, he dutifully lay on the floor with his feet in the air, ready for a nice belly rub.

Arty's Wagging Heart

A Story By Kayla Orlando

Once upon a time, in a cosy neighbourhood, there lived a cheerful Pembroke Welsh Corgi named Arty. Arty was a bundle of energy with a heart full of love, but there was something different about him – his tail was missing, a small detail that set him apart from the other dogs in the park.

Arty loved going to the park to play with his furry friends. However, every time he tried to join in their games, he felt a bit left out. The other dogs would wag their tails happily while chasing each other, but Arty's stubby tail couldn't join the dance.

One sunny day, Arty decided he wanted to be just like the other dogs. He tried to attach a fluffy toy to his tail with a ribbon, hoping it would make him more like his tail-wagging pals. As he trotted into the park, he felt a mix of excitement and nervousness.

But instead of fitting in, the other dogs tilted their heads, puzzled by Arty's makeshift tail. They whispered among themselves, and a little Poodle named Bella said, "You can't pretend to have a tail, Arty."

Feeling a bit disheartened, Arty retreated to a quiet corner. That's when a wise old Labrador named Max approached him. Max had seen it all and understood how Arty felt.

"Arty, my friend, don't try to be someone you're not," Max said with a gentle smile. "Your tail might be short, but your heart is big. Embrace what makes you special, and others will see the joy within you."

Arty pondered Max's words and decided to give it another try. This time, instead of pretending, he approached the other dogs with a genuine smile and a wag of his little tail stub. To his surprise, the dogs welcomed him with open paws.

As they played together, Arty realised that his uniqueness made him stand out in the best way possible. The other dogs soon saw the joy in Arty's wag, even if it was a bit different from theirs. They learned that tails come in all shapes and sizes, just like friends.

From that day on, Arty embraced his individuality, and the park became a place of laughter, joy, and acceptance. The other dogs no longer focused on the length of his tail but on the happiness he brought to their playtime.

And so, under the golden sun and a sky filled with fluffy clouds, Arty and his newfound friends wagged their tails together, celebrating the wonderful tapestry of differences that made each dog unique.

And as the sun dipped below the horizon, casting warm hues across the park, Arty curled up with his friends, knowing that being true to yourself is the key to finding love and acceptance – a lesson that echoed through the hearts of dogs and humans alike, making bedtime a time of comfort, warmth, and dreams filled with wagging tails.

A Scoop of Joy

A Story By Melodie Tardif-Faessel

On a bright and sunny day, in a quaint seaside town, there lived a 10-week-old light Golden Retriever named Elliot. Elliot, with his soft, golden fur and curious, sparkling eyes, was about to experience a delightful first – his very first ice cream.

Elliot spent his days exploring the world with wide-eyed wonder, and today was no different. He was accompanied by his best friend, Bonnie, a playful and loving Labrador. Together, they made a charming pair, with Elliot's youthful enthusiasm perfectly complemented by Bonnie's gentle guidance.

As they trotted down the bustling streets, Elliot's nose twitched with excitement. The aromas of the sea mingled with the myriad scents of the town, creating an intoxicating bouquet of smells that captivated the young pup. It was then that they stumbled upon a quaint ice cream parlour, famous among locals for its unique flavours.

The owner, a kind-hearted man with a soft spot for dogs, noticed the two furry friends at his doorstep. With a smile, he offered them a special treat – a scoop of peanut butter and banana-flavoured ice cream, a canine-friendly delight. Elliot's eyes widened in anticipation, his tail wagging uncontrollably.

As the owner gently placed the bowl on the ground, Elliot hesitated for a moment, his nose hovering over the creamy concoction. With an encouraging nudge from Bonnie, he took his first lick. The cold, sweet sensation was unlike anything he had ever experienced. The flavours of peanut butter and banana exploded in his mouth, sending waves of joy through his little body.

Bonnie, an experienced ice cream connoisseur, joined in, savouring her share with contented licks. The two friends sat side by side, enjoying their frozen treats under the warm sun, their faces smeared with evidence of their indulgence.

Once the ice cream adventure was over, Elliot and Bonnie continued their day out towards the beach. The beach was a symphony of sights and sounds – the rhythmic crashing of waves, the laughter of children building sandcastles, and the distant calls of seagulls.

Elliot, experiencing the beach for the first time, was overjoyed. He dashed towards the water, his paws kicking up sand as he went. Bonnie, ever the protective companion, followed close behind, ensuring Elliot's safety. Together, they splashed in the shallow waves, chased after seagulls, and dug holes in the soft, warm sand.

As the sun began to set, painting the sky in hues of orange and pink, Elliot and Bonnie lay on the sand, exhausted but content. They watched the horizon, where the sea met the sky, and the world seemed to stand still in perfect harmony.

Elliot's first ice cream experience, followed by a playful afternoon at the beach, was more than just a day out; it was a memory that would stay with him forever. It was a day of firsts, of friendship, and of the simple joys that life has to offer.

As they made their way back home, the cool evening breeze gently ruffled their fur. Elliot looked up at Bonnie with adoration. He knew that with a friend like her by his side, every day was an adventure waiting to happen. The little Golden Retriever, with his heart full of happiness, trotted home, eagerly anticipating the many adventures that lay ahead.

Dakota the Mountain Pup

A Story By Gemma Coombs

On a chilly January day, high up on a mountain in Romania, a litter of puppies was born. A few days later, their mother, in her wisdom, decided to venture down the mountain to find some food for her puppies, but she never returned. Her puppies were left behind on that mountain with no one to look after them.

Then, out of the shadows, appeared a figure who took these puppies and cared for them. However, that couldn't last forever; these puppies needed homes of their own.

The puppies spent their days perfecting their "adopt me" faces, and quickly, they all found the perfect homes for themselves, all except for one.

Now, this puppy wasn't the biggest, and she definitely wasn't the bravest, but she knew she wanted to be loved. So, she summoned all her courage and tried to be brave so that she would eventually find her "forever home," and she did.

The time came for the long journey across Europe to their new homes. The ride seemed to go on forever, and none of the puppies knew what awaited them. They had only known each other and had never been separated until this moment. They all had to be as brave as they could be, but it was especially challenging for the little puppy.

She was scared, thinking, 'Where am I going? Where are my brothers and sisters?' All of a sudden, the door flung open, and the sun was shining on her face. 'Where am I? Who are you?' she thought as she was placed into the arms of her new parents, who already loved her very much, and driven to her new home.

Finally, she had a home all of her own, with her own bed and teddies. No longer did she have to share food. She went on adventures in the South of England and made new friends (the best way she knows how). For a puppy who once believed that a loving home was only ever a fairy tale, it had now become her reality because dreams do really come true, especially for Dakota, the Mountain Pup.

A Tail of Two Thrones

A Story By Adele Pember

Once upon a time in a kingdom far, far away (well, not that far, it was just down the road), lived a dog so pampered and adored, he was nothing short of canine royalty. This was Charlie, or as he preferred, King Charles.

King Charles had a life many dogs could only dream of. From the fluffiest beds to the tastiest treats, he had it all. His realm extended from the cosy corners of the living room to the farthest reaches of the back garden, and his subjects—his loving family—were ever at his beck and call, attending to his royal desires. Walks were royal parades unless it rained, in which case they were promptly cancelled as he expected to be carried like a furry prince. At night, he demanded to be lifted onto the human's bed with all the ceremony of a king ascending his throne. And if, by some misfortune, a dog-sitter dared to enter his realm, King Charles would promptly exile himself upstairs – after all, he couldn't possibly spend his time with peasants!

King Charles' love for treats was legendary. He would woof his royal demands for more food, and if his calls were unanswered, he would embark on a quest to find more, because a king should never go hungry.

One day, a whirlwind named Minnie entered King Charles' kingdom. Minnie was a small, skinny dog with lanky legs that seemed to have a mind of their own. Her fur was matted, and she carried the aroma of her previous life on the streets of Romania. She was a ball of energy, goofy and completely un-ladylike, the polar opposite of the regal King Charles. Minnie communicated exclusively in Romanian woofs, a quirky language unfamiliar to the distinguished King Charles. But in a grand gesture of royal benevolence, King Charles welcomed her to his court.

Minnie quickly adapted to her new royal life, her goofiness and whirlwind antics bringing a new kind of chaos to the orderly kingdom. She assumed the title of Queen of the House, a rule marked by counter-surfing, exuberant barking at innocent passersby, and a delightful disregard for royal etiquette. King Charles, initially unsure about this unruly addition, soon found himself questioning the wisdom of his subjects.

One day, King Charles spotted a tantalising bag of treats on a desk. He let out a commanding woof but no human servant appeared to fulfil his demand. Suddenly Minnie leapt with the grace of a gazelle (if gazelles were particularly goofy and uncoordinated), she bounded onto the desk. Her long, lanky legs sent the treats cascading down in a glorious, edible avalanche. They feasted together, Minnie gobbling treats with a fervour that King Charles found both endearing and horrifying.

As Charlie looked into Minnie's eyes, he saw a reflection of a life so different from his own. He had been pampered since puppyhood, while Minnie had known nothing but hardship. It was then that King Charles realised the true meaning of royalty – it wasn't about the treats or the fluffy beds, but about sharing your kingdom with others.

From that day on, Minnie was not just a queen by title, but by heart. She settled in, making herself comfortable wherever she pleased, happy just to be part of a family. Charlie, despite his royal quirks, was a lovable character at heart. He still demanded to be lifted onto beds and would give the death stare if a walk didn't meet his high standards. But deep down, he had learned the joy of sharing his kingdom with another.

King Charles and Queen Minnie became the talk of the town, a duo that brought laughter and love into their home. And as for those treats on the desk? Well, let's just say they learned to keep them a little higher up – royalty or not, some habits never change!

A Tail of Unlikely Friendship

A Story By Rachel Brown

In a little Welsh village with a square quite small,
Lived Gracie the Great Dane who was VERY tall.

People were scared, kept their distance with fear,
But Gracie just longed for a friend to draw near.

In a tucked-away corner, where whispers would play,
Was Mabel, a mouse, with a heart in dismay.

Folks were uneasy, their nerves tied in a knot,
But Mabel just longed for a friend she'd not got.

One day, fate stepped in, their paths intertwined,
Gracie and Mabel, an odd pair you would find.

With a woof and a squeak, they greeted so sweet,
Two lonely hearts, their friendship a treat.

Gracie's paws, oh so big, carried Mabel with grace,
A mouse and a Dane, an unlikely embrace.

Through laughter and play, they showed the town wide,
That friendship's not bound by looks on the outside.

Slowly but surely, the town came to see,
It's not about size or how different we be.

With Gracie and Mabel, a lesson they learned,
In friendship and love, true colours are earned.

Now the town that was once full of worry and fright,
Had a circle of friends, in the day and the night.

A great lesson was learned, everyone could now see,
That in friendship's embrace, all creatures are free.

Spots Of Confidence

A Story By Lorren Francis

Once upon a time, there was an anxious Dalmatian named Loki. He was covered in black and white spots that made him stand out from all the other dogs in the park. Whenever Loki went out for walkies, he felt nervous around the other dogs as none of them had spots like him.

Loki would shy away from playing and hide behind the benches or even bark at other dogs to scare them away. One summer's day, Loki's family decided to take him on a drive to the countryside to get away from the town for a while. As they drove through the rolling green hills, Loki gazed out of the window feeling gloomy.

When they stopped to let Loki out for a walk, he slowly wandered down a muddy trail that led to a large, rolling field. Loki stopped and stared in awe - grazing lazily in the meadow was a huge herd of spotted cows! He had only seen brown cows before! Their black and white splotches mirrored Loki's own polka dots.

Cautiously, Loki approached the herd, timidly wagging his tail. He was amazed to be around other spotted animals for the first time. Loki met a kind old cow named Daisy, who welcomed Loki with a gentle "Moo." "You look glum, dear. What troubles you?" asked Daisy in a soothing, motherly voice. "I'm just different from the other dogs with my spots," said Loki sadly. "They never want to play with me."

Daisy nodded slowly. "Nonsense. Your spots make you special. We cows embrace our patches, and there's always room in our herd for those who are different. You just have to moo-ve past your worries." Loki felt comforted by Daisy's wisdom. He spent the rest of the afternoon following Daisy as she grazed calmly across the meadow. Loki even tried nibbling on some fresh green grass alongside the cows but couldn't see what the fuss was about.

As the sun began to set, Loki knew it was time to return home with his family. He was filled with joy after spending time with the herd but felt sad to leave his new friends. Loki gazed back longingly across the grassy meadow at the grazing cows. Daisy came over and gave Loki an affectionate nuzzle. "Remember, woofy one, you are special because of your spots, not in spite of them," Daisy said warmly. Loki knew he would return to visit the meadow again soon. For the first time, he felt proud of his spotted coat and realised it made him unique, not weird. From that day forward, Loki carried his head high, no longer anxious or alone because of his one-of-a-kind spots.

The Journey

A Story By Laura McElroy

The black waves crashed against the wooden hull, echoing inside Lupo's head like thunder. His nails scarred the floor as his paws splayed beneath him, scrambling for grip as the ship lurched in an attempt to stay upright in the storm engulfing them.

"Lupo! Get out here, Buddy!" The shout travelled to Lupo from the deck above, beside the sound of hard footsteps striding back and forth, each step splashing in the rising flood. Heading for the stairs, Lupo's usually smooth gait was unsteady, but his tried and trusted sea legs led him out and into the blustering winds.

Lupo slid across the rocking deck, slamming abruptly into the edge, sea water up to his belly and rising rapidly. He leaped up so his front paws and head could see ahead, and his tail began wagging when he spotted white sand, not two miles away. They'd made it.

The small boat shifted slowly into the soft sand, the strong waves making short work of the trip. Lupo jumped out to swim the final few metres, not letting his head bob underneath the sea water as he swam. He looked down at his paws as he padded through the sand, watching the white mix into with his curly black fur. He got further inland where the sand felt dryer and shook the water from his coat, looking up at his best friend - Henry, they call him - as he followed suit, wringing out his barely-there shirt and throwing it over his shoulder. His skin was sunburnt - the weather here felt like a different season every few hours - and his eyes looked tired. He pulled a thin and ragged parchment from his back pocket, unrolling it, furrowing his dark brows and running a frustrated hand through his beard. Following his compass as a guide, Henry whistled for Lupo to follow and headed away from the stormy white beach towards the dark tree line.

Lupo cautiously tiptoed into the shadow of the rainforest. He usually enjoyed when the ground squelched between his paws, but something didn't feel quite right this time. The urge to roll onto his back was there, but something stopped him. The rainforest had been alive with sound as they'd approached. Noise saturated the air around them, filling every breath and masking their light footfalls. Croaking frogs, shrieking birds, and buzzing insects surrounded them. Until Henry stepped over a branch, catching it with his back foot. The crack shattered the world around them, and, for a moment, everything stopped. The silence was deafening, and something didn't smell right. Lupo silently lifted his nose into the air, taking in the scent of the forest, letting the aroma travel to the back of his throat. His eyes opened with a start, and his body froze. Looking over at Henry - who also stood very still and silent - Lupo slowly crept towards a large rock leaning over the small stream running through the forest, making sure to avoid the amber gaze he felt following his movements. With one more look towards Henry, Lupo waited for his friend's small nod, and threw his head back and howled. With a start, the large predator ran in the opposite direction. No doubt surprised by the unfamiliar noise on this deserted island rather than afraid, for this moment at least, they were safe.

Henry climbed onto the large rock and sat with his legs dangling over the edge, hand raised to his forward, squinting as the rain slowed and the sun started to reveal more of the scenery around them. Lupo moved to sit next to him, and settled with his head in Henry's lap, looking up and waiting for his reward.

Henry dug into his pockets and pulled out some jerky, breaking it in half so they could share. It was all he had with him. He looked again at the parchment, impossibly unaffected by the wet weather, remaining clear as the day Henry found it. Lupo wasn't sure where they were headed or why, but he knew he was having the best time getting there. He rolled onto his back, looking at the underside of Henry's chin although it might tell him more.

After what could have been years but was probably only a handful of minutes, Lupo's chocolate brown eyes fluttered open, noticing the sky hadn't changed much, maybe it hadn't been that long really. He stretched, and jumped down to have a drink from the stream.

"Biiiig stretch," came the voice from above him. People are weird, Lupo thought. Henry followed him, jumping down and scooping some water for himself, then set off again with purpose, deeper still.

The rainforest felt safer in the daylight, and Lupo even let himself have a roll in the stinky bog. He ran around, stretching legs and jumping over the twisted roots of the mangroves. Henry threw him some sticks, but this part of their adventure felt different than before. Henry walked with more purpose than usual, his pace quickened - he could almost keep up with Lupo.

When the pair had covered what Lupo thought must have been the entire island and back, his legs starting to ache. They had come out the other side of the forest, and found themselves in a dry clearing. It looked and tasted like this part of the island hadn't seen water in a long time. Lupo found this strange, knowing they had just been in a storm only hours before. Maybe they really had been walking for days. He asked Henry for a drink, scratching a paw not entirely gently against the back of Henry's leg.

"Just wait, Lupo... I think we've found it!" Henry looked around him in every direction, looking for something Lupo couldn't guess at. Henry suddenly stopped, bouncing up and down on the spot, a wide smile spreading across his face.

"DIG, LUPO! DIG!"

Paying it paw-ward..

A True Story By Sophie Manners

Somewhere far away in a distant land, a little dog without a name was found. He cowered in the shadows of a busy street, in a rusty cage on the floor of a market, being sold for his meat. The wind and rain were cold, and the little dog was hungry. But one day, a passerby with a kind heart noticed and offered him a bite to eat.

Dirty, hungry, and hurting, this little dog experienced kindness for the first time. With gentle hands and a soothing voice, the dog was lifted from the darkness. His rescuer promised that he had a forever family waiting for him, that he was already loved, and that he would be perfectly fine.

They carried him back to an animal shelter, where he was fed a warm meal and allowed to go at his own pace. He wasn't alone; there were lots of other dogs there to welcome him and show him around this new safe place. Some were thin, some were bald, some were grey, and some were old. There were even pets who had been abandoned in the cold. The sanctuary offered more than four walls and shelter; it was a refuge of compassion, with incredible volunteers who never gave up on the

many animals in need and made them feel better. They gave love freely where so many dogs had been let down and heartbroken. Day by day, they built bonds, mended injuries, and gave out hundreds of cuddles, teaching them to love and trust humans again.

And his rescuer kept their word of course! There really was a woman out there with her heart set on that sad little dog from the moment she saw him. She named him Teddie and donated towards his care and upkeep. She promised to have a spot on the sofa for him once he was well enough to travel.

Through the tapestry of time, the path of this little dog and a family far away joined together. Both Teddie and his mum were counting down the days until his 'freedom flight' from China to his new home where he'll be loved forever.

Slowly, the little dog regained his strength with each step he took, fighting against the sickness that he'd caught on the street. As his wounded soul mended, it revealed a fiery cocker spaniel spirit - Teddie found his bark again and his world felt complete.

Today, Teddie lives on a farm in Somerset, England, where he chases the birds through the fields and happily eats apples off the orchard trees.

Now a model for luxury dog beds, Teddie is an ambassador for Ralph & Co's 'spoil a dog, save a dog' initiative. It actively supports incredible animal rescues, like Harbin SHS, who are doing something positive. The shelter saved Teddie, and many animals like him, from a terrible fate. Their hope is to encourage more people to support their mission and contribute to something great.

The actions of one kind passerby who stepped in and saved a sad little dog led to years of happiness for Teddie and his new family, which they'll never forget. His rescuer gave him more than freedom but also a bed to snuggle in, a family to play with, and the opportunity to learn what it means to be a pet. Never underestimate the impact your actions can have. Through small acts of kindness, you can change someone's future.

As Teddie entered his newfound life, he carried with him the reminder of that stranger's kindness, their choice to intervene and change his entire world for the better. No longer destined for the dinner plate, this little spaniel is now his mum's greatest companion.

Teddie and his family would like to thank all the volunteers who dedicate their time and hearts to him and the rest of the homeless and abused animals around the world. These heroes are the unseen golden thread that weaves through the happy adoption stories, proving that small acts of kindness can change many lives.

Printed in Great Britain
by Amazon

38342541R00030